SCREW
CALM
AND
GET
ANGRY

SCREW CALM AND GET ANGRY

RESIGNED ADVICE FOR HARD TIMES

Andrews McMeel
Publishing, LLC

Kansas City • Sydney • London

10 11 12 13 14 TEN 10 9 8 7 6 5 4 3 2

ISBN: 978-0-7407-9952-5

Library of Congress Control Number: 2010931443

First published in Great Britain by
Ebury Press, an imprint of Ebury Publishing,
a Random House Group company

www.andrewsmcmeel.com

Attention: Schools and Businesses
Andrews McMeel books are available at quantity discounts with bulk purchase for educational, business, or sales promotional use. For information, please write to: Special Sales Department, Andrews McMeel Publishing, LLC, 1130 Walnut Street, Kansas City, Missouri 64106.

IF WE SEE LIGHT AT THE END OF THE TUNNEL, IT IS THE LIGHT OF THE ONCOMING TRAIN.

Robert Lowell

CONTENTS

INTRODUCTION

Civilization

Happiness

Unhappiness

Deceit

Hypocrisy

Morality

Rat Race

Curmudgeon

Anger

Protest

INTRODUCTION

Our stiff upper lip can last only for so long. Disgruntled grumpiness, whispered complaint, and incensed anger are now in order. "This is ridiculous," "I'd like to speak to the manager," and "We're all going to hell in a handcart" are the traditional battle cries. And in our current state of economic misery and political distrust, surely there is a limit to just how much keeping calm and carrying on a gentleman or lady might be expected to undertake. You may very well find that getting your dander up might be the only way to get things changed around here.

To help you achieve a new state of mild motivation, *Screw Calm and Get Angry* brings together several centuries of embattled and embittered epithets. We've combed the world to reveal cynicism and resignation from Napoleon and Voltaire to

Abraham Lincoln and Charles M. Schulz to Benjamin Disraeli and George Bernard Shaw. It would seem that across the world and across the centuries, there is plenty of evidence to suggest you're not alone in bemoaning the way the odds are stacked. Fear not the cynic and the curmudgeon, for he or she is by definition not a true misanthrope but usually a romantic in a bunker. Here is someone who is simply protecting his or her true ideals from the harsh realities encountered on a daily basis. The cynic is in fact the one who cares the most. So the purpose of this collection of resigned advice is not to make you even more bitter but maybe to offer a temporary salve in these unyielding hard times, a few well-turned grumbles and whines to help release a little pent-up steam. Perhaps these comforting negative thoughts might steer you to a more nourishing, positive future. For surely, if we manage to dodge the oncoming train, there is a sunlit end to the tunnel somewhere ahead?

THE WORD "POLITICS" IS DERIVED FROM THE WORD "POLY," MEANING "MANY," AND THE WORD "TICKS," MEANING "BLOOD SUCKING PARASITES."

Larry Hardiman

POLITICS, N. STRIFE OF INTERESTS MASQUERADING AS A CONTEST OF PRINCIPLES. THE CONDUCT OF PUBLIC AFFAIRS FOR PRIVATE ADVANTAGE.

Ambrose Bierce

MY CHOICE
EARLY IN LIFE
WAS EITHER TO BE
A PIANO-PLAYER
IN A WHOREHOUSE
OR A POLITICIAN.
AND TO TELL THE
TRUTH, THERE'S
HARDLY ANY
DIFFERENCE.

Harry S. Truman

POLITICS IS SUPPOSED TO BE THE SECOND-OLDEST PROFESSION. I HAVE COME TO REALIZE THAT IT BEARS A VERY CLOSE RESEMBLANCE TO THE FIRST.

Ronald Reagan

POLITICS IS THE ART OF LOOKING FOR TROUBLE, FINDING IT, MISDIAGNOSING IT, AND THEN MISAPPLYING THE WRONG REMEDIES.

Groucho Marx

POLITICS IS PERHAPS THE ONLY PROFESSION FOR WHICH NO PREPARATION IS THOUGHT NECESSARY.

Robert Louis Stevenson

WHENEVER A MAN HAS CAST A LONGING EYE ON OFFICES, A ROTTENNESS BEGINS IN HIS CONDUCT.

Thomas Jefferson

I HAVE COME TO THE CONCLUSION THAT POLITICS ARE TOO SERIOUS A MATTER TO BE LEFT TO THE POLITICIANS.

Charles de Gaulle

WE HANG THE PETTY THIEVES AND APPOINT THE GREAT ONES TO PUBLIC OFFICE.

Aesop

HE KNOWS NOTHING AND THINKS HE KNOWS EVERYTHING. THAT POINTS CLEARLY TO A POLITICAL CAREER.

George Bernard Shaw

POLITICIANS ARE THE SAME ALL OVER. THEY PROMISE TO BUILD A BRIDGE EVEN WHERE THERE IS NO RIVER.

Nikita Khrushchev

THERE ARE NO TRUE FRIENDS IN POLITICS. WE ARE ALL SHARKS, CIRCLING AND WAITING FOR TRACES OF BLOOD TO APPEAR IN THE WATER.

Alan Clark

INSTEAD OF
GIVING A POLITICIAN
THE KEYS TO THE
CITY, IT MIGHT BE
BETTER TO CHANGE
THE LOCKS.

Doug Larson

IT IS INEXCUSABLE FOR SCIENTISTS TO TORTURE ANIMALS; LET THEM MAKE THEIR EXPERIMENTS ON JOURNALISTS AND POLITICIANS.

Henrik Ibsen

A POLITICIAN IS AN ANIMAL WHO CAN SIT ON A FENCE AND YET KEEP BOTH EARS TO THE GROUND.

H. L. Mencken

THE ART OF
POLITICS

POLITICAL SUCCESS IS THE ABILITY, WHEN THE INEVITABLE OCCURS, TO GET CREDIT FOR IT.

Laurence J. Peter

IN POLITICS . . .
NEVER RETREAT,
NEVER RETRACT . . .
NEVER ADMIT
A MISTAKE.

Napoleon Bonaparte

POLITICS IS THE ART OF PREVENTING PEOPLE FROM STICKING THEIR NOSES IN THINGS THAT ARE PROPERLY THEIR BUSINESS.

Paul Valéry

IF YOU CAN'T CONVINCE THEM, CONFUSE THEM.

Harry S. Truman

**UNDER DEMOCRACY
ONE PARTY ALWAYS
DEVOTES ITS CHIEF
ENERGIES TO TRYING
TO PROVE THAT THE
OTHER PARTY IS UNFIT
TO RULE—AND BOTH
COMMONLY SUCCEED
AND ARE RIGHT.**

H. L. Mencken

**APPARENTLY,
A DEMOCRACY IS
A PLACE WHERE
NUMEROUS ELECTIONS
ARE HELD AT GREAT
COST WITHOUT
ISSUES AND WITH
INTERCHANGEABLE
CANDIDATES.**

Gore Vidal

THE WHOLE DREAM OF DEMOCRACY IS TO RAISE THE PROLETARIAN TO THE LEVEL OF STUPIDITY ATTAINED BY THE BOURGEOIS.

Gustave Flaubert

ONE OF THE SYMPTOMS OF AN APPROACHING NERVOUS BREAKDOWN IS THE BELIEF THAT ONE'S WORK IS TERRIBLY IMPORTANT.

Bertrand Russell

**BY WORKING
FAITHFULLY EIGHT
HOURS A DAY, YOU
MAY EVENTUALLY
GET TO BE A BOSS
AND WORK TWELVE
HOURS A DAY.**

Robert Frost

A LIFE SPENT IN
CONSTANT LABOR
IS A LIFE WASTED,
SAVE A MAN BE
SUCH A FOOL AS
TO REGARD A
FULSOME OBITUARY
NOTICE AS
AMPLE REWARD.

George Jean Nathan

FAR FROM IDLENESS BEING THE ROOT OF ALL EVIL, IT IS RATHER THE ONLY TRUE GOOD.

Søren Kierkegaard

A GOOD RULE
OF THUMB IS IF
YOU'VE MADE IT
TO THIRTY-FIVE
AND YOUR JOB
STILL REQUIRES
YOU TO WEAR A
NAME TAG, YOU'VE
MADE A SERIOUS
VOCATIONAL ERROR.

Dennis Miller

THE BEST TIME
TO START THINKING
ABOUT YOUR
RETIREMENT IS
BEFORE THE
BOSS DOES.

Anonymous

ONLY TWO THINGS
ARE INFINITE,
THE UNIVERSE AND
HUMAN STUPIDITY,
AND I'M NOT SURE
ABOUT THE FORMER.

Albert Einstein

CABBAGE: A FAMILIAR KITCHEN-GARDEN VEGETABLE ABOUT AS LARGE AND WISE AS A MAN'S HEAD.

Ambrose Bierce

A GREAT MANY
PEOPLE THINK THEY
ARE THINKING WHEN
THEY ARE MERELY
REARRANGING THEIR
PREJUDICES.

William James

THE ONLY REASON SOME PEOPLE GET LOST IN THOUGHT IS BECAUSE IT'S UNFAMILIAR TERRITORY.

Paul Fix

**THAT MEN
DO NOT LEARN
VERY MUCH FROM
THE LESSONS OF
HISTORY IS THE
MOST IMPORTANT
OF ALL THE LESSONS
THAT HISTORY HAS
TO TEACH.**

Aldous Huxley

THE AVERAGE MAN'S OPINIONS ARE MUCH LESS FOOLISH THAN THEY WOULD BE IF HE THOUGHT FOR HIMSELF.

Bertrand Russell

HALF THE WORLD IS COMPOSED OF IDIOTS, THE OTHER HALF OF PEOPLE CLEVER ENOUGH TO TAKE INDECENT ADVANTAGE OF THEM.

Walter Kerr

WHEN A STUPID MAN IS DOING SOMETHING HE IS ASHAMED OF, HE ALWAYS DECLARES THAT IT IS HIS DUTY.

George Bernard Shaw

WISE MEN TALK BECAUSE THEY HAVE SOMETHING TO SAY; FOOLS, BECAUSE THEY HAVE TO SAY SOMETHING.

Plato

MONEY

MONEY:
THERE'S NOTHING
IN THE WORLD SO
DEMORALIZING
AS MONEY.

Sophocles

NEVER SPEND YOUR MONEY BEFORE YOU HAVE IT.

Thomas Jefferson

I HAVE
ENOUGH MONEY
TO LAST ME THE
REST OF MY LIFE,
UNLESS I BUY
SOMETHING.

Jackie Mason

HE THAT IS OF
THE OPINION
MONEY WILL DO
EVERYTHING
MAY WELL BE
SUSPECTED OF
DOING EVERYTHING
FOR MONEY.

Benjamin Franklin

NOTHING IS AS IRRITATING AS THE CHAP WHO CHATS PLEASANTLY TO YOU WHILE HE'S OVERCHARGING YOU.

Kin Hubbard

MANY OF THE THINGS YOU CAN COUNT DON'T COUNT. MANY OF THE THINGS YOU CAN'T COUNT REALLY COUNT.

Albert Einstein

THE EASIEST
WAY FOR YOUR
CHILDREN TO LEARN
ABOUT MONEY IS
FOR YOU NOT
TO HAVE ANY.

Katharine Whitehorn

**OUR INCOMES ARE
LIKE OUR SHOES;
IF TOO SMALL,
THEY GALL AND
PINCH US, BUT IF
TOO LARGE, THEY
CAUSE US TO
STUMBLE AND TRIP.**

Charles Caleb Colton

MONEY CANNOT BUY HEALTH, BUT I'D SETTLE FOR A DIAMOND-STUDDED WHEELCHAIR.

Dorothy Parker

WHEN YOU HAVE TOLD ANYONE YOU HAVE LEFT HIM A LEGACY, THE ONLY DECENT THING TO DO IS TO DIE AT ONCE.

Samuel Butler

THE FIRST RULE OF BUSINESS IS: DO OTHER MEN FOR THEY WOULD DO YOU.

Charles Dickens

IN MODERN BUSINESS IT IS NOT THE CROOK WHO IS TO BE FEARED MOST, IT IS THE HONEST MAN WHO DOESN'T KNOW WHAT HE IS DOING.

William Wordsworth

BUSINESS IS A GOOD GAME—LOTS OF COMPETITION AND A MINIMUM OF RULES. YOU KEEP SCORE WITH MONEY.

Nolan Bushnell

**CRIMINAL:
A PERSON WITH
PREDATORY
INSTINCTS WHO
HAS NOT SUFFICIENT
CAPITAL TO FORM
A CORPORATION.**

Howard Scott

THE DEFINITION OF A CONSULTANT: SOMEONE WHO BORROWS YOUR WATCH, TELLS YOU THE TIME, AND THEN CHARGES YOU FOR THE PRIVILEGE.

A letter in The Times

NOTHING IS ILLEGAL IF A HUNDRED BUSINESSMEN DECIDE TO DO IT, AND THAT'S TRUE ANYWHERE IN THE WORLD.

Andrew Young

ADVERTISING MAY BE DESCRIBED AS THE SCIENCE OF ARRESTING THE HUMAN INTELLIGENCE LONG ENOUGH TO GET MONEY FROM IT.

Stephen Leacock

**BUSINESS?
IT'S QUITE SIMPLE.
IT'S OTHER
PEOPLE'S MONEY.**

Alexandre Dumas

BANKS

THEY USUALLY HAVE TWO TELLERS IN MY LOCAL BANK, EXCEPT WHEN IT'S VERY BUSY, WHEN THEY HAVE ONE.

Rita Rudner

**THE MODERN
BANKING SYSTEM
MANUFACTURES MONEY
OUT OF NOTHING.
THE PROCESS IS
PERHAPS THE MOST
ASTOUNDING PIECE
OF SLEIGHT-OF-HAND
THAT WAS EVER
INVENTED. BANKING
WAS CONCEIVED IN
INEQUITY AND**

**BORN IN SIN. . . .
BUT IF YOU WANT
TO CONTINUE TO
BE SLAVES OF THE
BANKERS AND PAY THE
COST OF YOUR OWN
SLAVERY, THEN LET THE
BANKERS CONTINUE TO
CREATE MONEY AND
CONTROL CREDIT.**

Josiah Charles Stamp

FINANCE IS THE ART OF PASSING MONEY FROM HAND TO HAND UNTIL IT FINALLY DISAPPEARS.

Robert W. Sarnoff

IF YOU OWE THE BANK $100, THAT'S YOUR PROBLEM. IF YOU OWE THE BANK $100 MILLION, THAT'S THE BANK'S PROBLEM.

J. Paul Getty

IF YOU THINK
NOBODY CARES
IF YOU'RE ALIVE,
TRY MISSING
A COUPLE OF
CAR PAYMENTS.

Earl Wilson

MY PROBLEM LIES IN RECONCILING MY GROSS HABITS WITH MY NET INCOME.

Errol Flynn

WE DIDN'T ACTUALLY OVERSPEND OUR BUDGET. THE ALLOCATION SIMPLY FELL SHORT OF OUR EXPENDITURE.

Keith Davis

**IT IS ONLY
BY NOT PAYING
ONE'S BILLS THAT
ONE CAN HOPE
TO LIVE IN THE
MEMORY OF THE
COMMERCIAL
CLASSES.**

Oscar Wilde

**WHEN I ASKED
MY ACCOUNTANT
IF ANYTHING COULD
GET ME OUT OF THIS
MESS I AM IN NOW,
HE THOUGHT FOR
A LONG TIME AND
SAID, "YES, DEATH
WOULD HELP."**

Robert Morley

A LOT OF PEOPLE BECOME PESSIMISTS FROM FINANCING OPTIMISTS.

C. T. Jones

A CREDITOR
IS WORSE THAN
A SLAVE-OWNER,
FOR THE MASTER
OWNS ONLY YOUR
PERSON, BUT A
CREDITOR OWNS
YOUR DIGNITY AND
CAN COMMAND IT.

Victor Hugo

THE MOMENT
YOU'RE BORN
YOU'RE DONE FOR.

Arnold Bennett

LIFE IS NOT SO BAD IF YOU HAVE PLENTY OF LUCK, A GOOD PHYSIQUE, AND NOT TOO MUCH IMAGINATION.

Christopher Isherwood

IF YOU WAKE UP AND YOU'RE NOT IN PAIN, YOU KNOW YOU'RE DEAD.

Russian proverb

THE SOONER
YOU FALL BEHIND,
THE MORE TIME
YOU'LL HAVE TO
CATCH UP!

Ogden's Law

THAT'S THE SECRET TO LIFE . . . REPLACE ONE WORRY WITH ANOTHER.

Charles M. Schulz

LIFE IS EASY
TO CHRONICLE
BUT BEWILDERING
TO PRACTICE.

E. M. Forster

I KNOW GOD
WILL NOT GIVE
ME ANYTHING
I CAN'T HANDLE.
I JUST WISH THAT
HE DIDN'T TRUST
ME SO MUCH.

Mother Teresa

CIVILIZATION

YOU CAN'T
SAY CIVILIZATION
DON'T ADVANCE . . .
FOR IN EVERY WAR
THEY KILL YOU
IN A NEW WAY.

Will Rogers

IN OUR CIVILIZATION,
AND UNDER OUR
REPUBLICAN FORM
OF GOVERNMENT,
INTELLIGENCE IS
SO HIGHLY HONORED
THAT IT IS REWARDED
BY EXEMPTION FROM
THE CARES OF OFFICE.

Ambrose Bierce

HAPPINESS

HAPPINESS, N. AN AGREEABLE SENSATION ARISING FROM CONTEMPLATING THE MISERY OF ANOTHER.

Ambrose Bierce

WE ARE MORE INTERESTED IN MAKING OTHERS BELIEVE WE ARE HAPPY THAN IN TRYING TO BE HAPPY OURSELVES.

François de La Rochefoucauld

WE WISH TO
BE HAPPIER THAN
OTHER PEOPLE, AND
THIS IS ALWAYS
DIFFICULT, FOR WE
BELIEVE OTHERS TO
BE HAPPIER THAN
THEY ARE.

*Charles-Louis de Secondat
baron de Montesquieu*

**POINT ME OUT
THE HAPPY MAN
AND I WILL
POINT YOU OUT
EITHER EGOTISM,
SELFISHNESS,
EVIL—OR ELSE
AN ABSOLUTE
IGNORANCE.**

Graham Greene

WHAT A WONDERFUL LIFE I'VE HAD! I ONLY WISH I'D REALIZED IT SOONER.

Colette

I'M AN OPTIMIST,
BUT I'M AN OPTIMIST
WHO CARRIES A
RAINCOAT.

Harold Wilson

CALL NO MAN
HAPPY 'TIL
HE IS DEAD.

Aeschylus

UNHAPPINESS

MEN WHO
ARE UNHAPPY,
LIKE MEN WHO
SLEEP BADLY,
ARE ALWAYS PROUD
OF THE FACT.

Bertrand Russell

ASK YOURSELF WHETHER YOU ARE HAPPY, AND YOU CEASE TO BE SO.

John Stuart Mill

NOBODY REALLY CARES IF YOU'RE MISERABLE, SO YOU MIGHT AS WELL BE HAPPY.

Cynthia Nelms

AND YET
TO EVERY
BAD THERE IS
A WORSE.

Thomas Hardy

DECEIT

WHEN WE ASK FOR ADVICE, WE ARE USUALLY LOOKING FOR AN ACCOMPLICE.

Marquis de la Grange

A GOVERNMENT THAT ROBS PETER TO PAY PAUL CAN ALWAYS DEPEND ON THE SUPPORT OF PAUL.

George Bernard Shaw

IT IS ALWAYS THE BEST POLICY TO SPEAK THE TRUTH—UNLESS, OF COURSE, YOU ARE AN EXCEPTIONALLY GOOD LIAR.

Jerome K. Jerome

LYING IS DONE WITH WORDS AND ALSO WITH SILENCE.

Adrienne Rich

HOW FORTUNATE
FOR LEADERS
THAT MEN DO
NOT THINK.

Adolf Hitler

HYPOCRISY

HYPOCRITE:
THE MAN WHO
MURDERED BOTH
HIS PARENTS . . .
PLEADED FOR
MERCY ON THE
GROUNDS THAT HE
WAS AN ORPHAN.

Abraham Lincoln

LET US BE GRATEFUL TO THE MIRROR FOR REVEALING TO US OUR APPEARANCE ONLY.

Samuel Butler

THE TRUE HYPOCRITE IS THE ONE WHO CEASES TO PERCEIVE HIS DECEPTION, THE ONE WHO LIES WITH SINCERITY.

André Gide

IT'S DISCOURAGING TO THINK HOW MANY PEOPLE ARE SHOCKED BY HONESTY AND HOW FEW BY DECEIT.

Noël Coward

WE HAVE, IN FACT, TWO KINDS OF MORALITY SIDE BY SIDE: ONE WHICH WE PREACH BUT DO NOT PRACTICE AND ANOTHER WHICH WE PRACTICE BUT SELDOM PREACH.

Bertrand Russell

THE MODERN CONSERVATIVE IS ENGAGED IN ONE OF MAN'S OLDEST EXERCISES IN MORAL PHILOSOPHY, THAT IS, THE SEARCH FOR A SUPERIOR MORAL JUSTIFICATION FOR SELFISHNESS.

J. K. Galbraith

NEVER KEEP UP WITH THE JONESES. DRAG THEM DOWN TO YOUR LEVEL. IT'S CHEAPER.

Quentin Crisp

NOTHING AGES YOUR CAR AS MUCH AS THE SIGHT OF YOUR NEIGHBOR'S NEW ONE.

Evan Esar

THE WORLD IS FULL
OF FOOLS AND
FAINT HEARTS; AND
YET EVERYONE HAS
COURAGE ENOUGH
TO BEAR THE
MISFORTUNES, AND
WISDOM ENOUGH TO
MANAGE THE AFFAIRS,
OF HIS NEIGHBOR.

Benjamin Franklin

WHENEVER A FRIEND SUCCEEDS, A LITTLE SOMETHING IN ME DIES.

Gore Vidal

CURMUDGEON

START OFF
EVERY DAY WITH
A SMILE AND GET
IT OVER WITH.

W. C. Fields

THE FIRST HALF OF OUR LIVES IS RUINED BY OUR PARENTS AND THE SECOND HALF BY OUR CHILDREN.

Clarence Darrow

I HAVE ALWAYS DISLIKED MYSELF AT ANY GIVEN MOMENT; THE TOTAL OF SUCH MOMENTS IS MY LIFE.

Cyril Connolly

A CYNIC IS
A MAN WHO,
WHEN HE SMELLS
FLOWERS, LOOKS
AROUND FOR
A COFFIN.

H. L. Mencken

IN CERTAIN TRYING
CIRCUMSTANCES,
URGENT
CIRCUMSTANCES,
DESPERATE
CIRCUMSTANCES,
PROFANITY
FURNISHES A
RELIEF DENIED
EVEN TO PRAYER.

Mark Twain

SPEAK WHEN
YOU ARE ANGRY
AND YOU WILL
MAKE THE BEST
SPEECH YOU WILL
EVER REGRET.

Ambrose Bierce

THERE MAY BE TIMES WHEN WE ARE POWERLESS TO PREVENT INJUSTICE, BUT THERE MUST NEVER BE A TIME WHEN WE FAIL TO PROTEST.

Elie Wiesel

**THE WORLD
IS A DANGEROUS
PLACE, NOT BECAUSE
OF THOSE WHO DO
EVIL BUT BECAUSE
OF THOSE WHO
LOOK ON AND
DO NOTHING.**

Albert Einstein

WE MUST
NOT ALLOW
OURSELVES TO
BECOME LIKE
THE SYSTEM
WE OPPOSE.

Archbishop Desmond Tutu

YOU MUST
DO THE THINGS
YOU THINK YOU
CANNOT DO.

Eleanor Roosevelt

**NEVER DOUBT THAT
A SMALL GROUP
OF THOUGHTFUL,
COMMITTED CITIZENS
CAN CHANGE THE
WORLD. INDEED,
IT IS THE ONLY
THING THAT
EVER HAS.**

Margaret Mead

TOO CROSS TO
THINK STRAIGHT?
YOU NEED: